ORCA
FOOTPRINTS

Fashion Forward

STRIVING FOR SUSTAINABLE STYLE

RAINA DELISLE

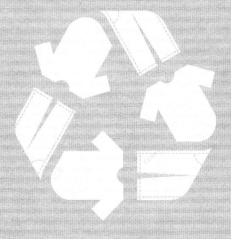

ORCA BOOK PUBLISHERS

T0038326

Published in Canada and the United States
in 2022 by Orca Book Publishers.
orcabook.com

Library and Archives Canada Cataloguing in Publication
Title: Fashion forward : striving for sustainable style / Raina Delisle.
Names: Delisle, Raina, author.
Series: Orca footprints.
Description: Series statement: Orca footprints |
Includes bibliographical references and index.
Identifiers: Canadiana (print) 20210165766 |
Canadiana (ebook) 20210166053 | ISBN 9781459825802 (hardcover) |
ISBN 9781459825819 (PDF) | ISBN 9781459825826 (EPUB)
Subjects: LCSH: Clothing trade—Social aspects. |
LCSH: Clothing trade—Environmental aspects. | LCSH: Fashion—
Social aspects. | LCSH: Fashion—Environmental aspects.
Classification: LCC HD9940.A2 D45 2022 | DDC j338.4/7687—dc23

Library of Congress Control Number: 2021934075

Summary: Part of the nonfiction Orca Footprints series for middle-
grade readers, this book explores the social and environmental issues
in the fashion industry and how kids can make it more sustainable.

Orca Book Publishers is committed to reducing the consumption
of nonrenewable resources in the making of our books. We make
every effort to use materials that support a sustainable future.

Orca Book Publishers gratefully acknowledges the support
for its publishing programs provided by the following
agencies: the Government of Canada, the Canada Council
for the Arts and the Province of British Columbia through
the BC Arts Council and the Book Publishing Tax Credit.

Front cover images by Vika Aleksandrova/Shutterstock.com
and MesquitaFMS/Getty Images
Back cover images by JGI/Jamie Grill/Getty Images,
FG Trade/Getty Images and Raina Delisle
Design by Teresa Bubela
Layout by Dahlia Yuen
Edited by Kirstie Hudson

Printed and bound in South Korea.

25 24 23 22 • 1 2 3 4

A boy walks through piles of fabric at a dyeing factory in India.
GRANT FAINT/GETTY IMAGES

For Ocea and Elodie

Contents

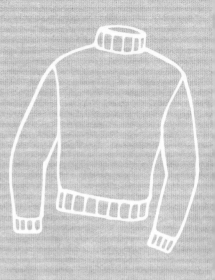

CHAPTER ONE
DRESSED TO IMPRESS

CHAPTER TWO
FASHION'S FOOTPRINT

CHAPTER THREE
TAKING ACTION ON FASHION

CHAPTER FOUR
BE A FASHION HERO

Introduction

Do you like my dress? It has narwhals on it and it was made by an ethical designer in my community, Smoking Lily.
TAYLOR ROADES/THE NARWHAL

More than a decade ago I made a New Year's resolution to stop buying clothes, shoes and accessories for one year. I was spending too much time and money shopping, and it wasn't making me happy. I was also concerned about the fashion industry's impact on people, animals and the planet. When I opened my crammed closet, I saw shirts that were falling apart after a few washes and high heels that I wore less often than Halloween costumes. Even worse, most things were made in countries where workers and the environment are often treated poorly.

After a successful year of avoiding malls and boutiques, I decided to try a year of shopping only in secondhand shops. I discovered a whole world of preloved fashion and realized that you don't have to sacrifice style for sustainability. Today I buy most of my family's wardrobe secondhand and from ethical companies. My kids and I also lend, borrow, swap and sell items.

Do you ever have a hard time deciding what to wear in the morning, like this boy? Me too!
VOLUROL/SHUTTERSTOCK.COM

I still haven't found zero-waste softball cleats or biodegradable dance leotards, but let me know if you do. Now that there are shoes made from pineapple leaves and bathing suits made from recycled plastic bottles, nothing would surprise me.

Before my New Year's resolution, I didn't know much about what went on behind the glitz and glamor of the fashion industry. I've since learned that there are lots of problems but also lots of people working hard on solutions. Put on a comfy outfit and come find out how you can be an ethical fashionista or fashionisto and inspire everyone around you.

CHAPTER ONE

Dressed to Impress

Every Child Matters

Students from Haahuupayak Elementary School in Port Alberni, BC, show their support for Orange Shirt Day, a day to remember the Indigenous children in Canada who were taken from their homes by government agents and placed in residential schools. Northern Secwepemc woman Phyllis Webstad inspired the event in 2013 after sharing her story of having her brand-new orange shirt taken away from her at residential school when she was six years old.

WHY ARE YOU WEARING THAT?

What are you wearing today? Does your outfit reflect your personal style, whether it's trendy, sporty, preppy, artsy or something totally unique? Are you dressed for the weather? You don't want to get caught in a snowstorm wearing sandals! Did you put on something special for an event? Maybe you're playing a baseball game, performing in a cultural celebration or going to a fancy party.

Clothing is one of our basic human needs, right up there with food and shelter, and it serves many important purposes. It protects our bodies, shows our support for causes, identifies us as members of groups and helps us express ourselves. Your clothes say a lot about you, but how much do you know about them?

Look at the label inside your favorite shirt. You can find out what country it was made in and what materials were used, but there's much more to the story. Who made it? How was it made? Is it ethical? In other words, were people, animals and the planet treated with respect while it was being made? It's difficult to answer these questions today, but it used to be much easier.

TRENDSETTERS

When a Nova Scotia boy wore a pink shirt on his first day of high school in 2007, he was teased by several other students. Two twelfth-grade students, Travis Price and David Shepherd, decided to do something about it. First they bought 75 pink shirts. Then they contacted their classmates through *social media* to tell them about their plan to turn the school into a sea of pink to show their support for the student. The next day Travis and David handed out the shirts and hundreds of students showed up in their own pink outfits. Not only did the students send a strong message to the kids who were being mean, but they also started an international anti-bullying movement that became known as Pink Shirt Day. Once a year kids wear pink shirts to school to show that they won't tolerate bullying. Today Pink Shirt Day is celebrated in more than 130 countries!

Travis Price, one of the founders of Pink Shirt Day, was bullied as a kid, which inspired him to stand up for others. Today he gives talks in schools about bullying prevention and mental health. TRAVIS PRICE

THE NAKED TRUTH

Did you know that people used to walk around naked all the time? How embarassing! No one knows for sure when or why our ancestors started wearing clothes, but it was sometime during the Ice Age, which started about 2.6 million years ago and ended about 11,700 years ago. Maybe people started feeling shy about being naked. Or perhaps they wanted to show off their personal style. The most likely explanation, however, is that they were cold. The climate has always gone through natural warming and cooling cycles. During the colder periods of the Ice Age, it may have felt like Queen Elsa had set off an eternal winter. People probably needed to cover up to survive.

Imagine you're shivering naked on the tundra, watching big, furry animals like bears and mammoths saunter by. What would you do? If you're like our ancestors, you'd kill them for their cozy coats. (Or ask an adult to do it for you.) The first clothes were likely loosely draped animal skins and furs, worn like superhero capes. People eventually figured out how to make

This linen dress, which is missing the bottom, is the world's oldest surviving woven garment. It was made more than 5,000 years ago!
COURTESY OF THE PETRIE MUSEUM OF EGYPTIAN ARCHAELOGY, UCL

needles out of animal bones and thread out of animal guts and plant fibers, and started crafting more complex clothing, such as parkas and pants. They also used tree bark to make clothing and accessories like hats. The first fashionistas and fashionistos even added some bling by sewing animal teeth and seashells onto their clothes.

Back then people couldn't collect closets full of clothes like we do today. They didn't even have closets! They were always moving from place to place in search of food and had to carry all their possessions with them. People made only the clothes they needed, their outfits decomposed when they were done with them and the animals they used were a *renewable resource*. Fashion started out as *sustainable*, but it didn't stay that way.

WEAVING THE WAY

How would you feel wearing a fur coat and leather pants in the middle of summer? It would be pretty hot and sweaty! When the Ice Age ended, the world warmed and animal skins and furs were no longer practical in some places. But people had become used to wearing clothes, so there was no going back to being naked. Fortunately they had already figured out how to remove fibers from plants, spin the fibers between their fingers to make thread and weave the thread into fabric by hand, kind of like finger-knitting. Eventually people made simple tools out of wood to help them make clothes—*spindles* for spinning and *looms* for weaving.

People started settling into communities to grow crops for food and clothes. Cotton, hemp and flax, which was used to make linen, were some of the earliest clothing crops, and they are still used today. People also started *domesticating* animals for food, clothing and labor. They sheared sheep to make wool, put cattle to work plowing fields and raised animals for their meat and hides. To soften hides and stop them from rotting, people came up with

A Peruvian woman weaves textiles using traditional techniques and naturally dyed wool from llamas, alpacas, guanacos and vicuñas.
HADYNYAH/GETTY IMAGES

an ingenious yet disgusting method called tanning. The hides were soaked in pee, rubbed with animal brains or poop and dunked in tannin, a substance found in tree bark. Imagine the smell! Natural materials like flowering plants, tree bark and sea-snail slime were used to dye textiles a rainbow of colors.

Ever wonder why it's called royal purple? In ancient times purple dye came from sea-snail slime and was so expensive that only royalty could afford it.
DOUBRAVKA POZAROVA/GETTY IMAGES

LET'S MAKE A TRADE

When you need new clothes, you can head to the shop, hand over some cash and walk out with your new duds. It wasn't so easy thousands of years ago. At first people swapped stuff with their neighbors. If they wanted something special that wasn't available nearby, they had to travel to find it. Demand for fabrics, precious metals and other luxury goods led to the development of long-distance trade routes.

The Silk Road was the most famous trade route of ancient times. Established more than 2,000 years ago, it linked China and Europe and played a major role in the exchange of goods and ideas. As the name of the route suggests, silk was one of the most important products on the market. Research shows Chinese people discovered how to make the luxurious fabric out of silk-worm cocoons more than 8,500 years ago and were determined to keep it a secret. Anyone busted for blabbing to a foreigner could be sentenced to death!

People often wear clothing and accessories for cultural reasons. For centuries girls from the Padaung tribe in Southeast Asia have worn brass collars around their necks to give them the appearance of long necks and show that they belong to the tribe.
NATTAWUT JAROENCHAI/SHUTTERSTOCK.COM

CLOTHING STYLES OF THE RICH AND FAMOUS

For thousands of years people made clothing entirely by hand. From planting crops to weaving fabrics to sewing garments, it took a ton of time and effort. Only the rich could afford to look fashionable, and poor people often had just one outfit. Fashion was used to reinforce the differences between *classes*. To show that they didn't have to work, Roman men wore silk togas and

Renaissance women wore elaborate gowns. In several societies it was even against the law for regular people to wear fancy clothes like purple togas, lace collars or fur coats. These **sumptuary laws** made sure that people didn't dress above their class or spend too much money on imported goods. Clothing was so highly valued that some people were even buried with their wardrobes so they could look rich and famous in the afterlife.

INDUSTRIAL STRENGTH

Making textiles and clothing got a whole lot faster and easier when inventors developed machines to do a lot of the work for us during the Industrial Revolution of the late 18th and early 19th century. These machines were powered by another important invention: the coal-burning steam engine. Textile and clothing factories started popping up across Europe and the United States, and coal mines got deeper and deeper. There were thousands of jobs to fill. **Immigrants** and farmers flocked to the cities in search of steady paychecks and better lives. Unfortunately that's not what they usually found.

In New York City in 1909, more than 20,000 garment workers, many of them teenage girls, went on strike for over two months to demand better pay, hours and working conditions.
GEORGE GRANTHAM BAIN COLLECTION/ LIBRARY OF CONGRESS

The factories and mines were typically dirty and dangerous, and companies often forced people to work long hours for poor pay. Many mothers used to stay home with the kids, but often the whole family had to go to work to earn enough money to survive, even kids your age. Children were given special jobs because of their small size, like crawling under spinning machines to collect cotton fluff and pulling wagons of coal up tight tunnels. The factories became known as **sweatshops** because people worked so hard they sweat a lot, and workers formed **unions** and went on **strike** to demand changes. These brave workers were often punished for speaking out, but they succeeded in changing many labor laws.

All this industrial activity, especially burning millions of tons of coal every year, polluted the environment. In some cities, the sun couldn't shine through the thick smoke. Nobody knew it at the time, but it was the beginning of human-caused *climate change*. Unlike the natural warming and cooling cycles of the Ice Age, human activity was now making the world warmer. Burning *fossil fuels* like coal releases *greenhouse gases* into the atmosphere. These gases trap the heat from the sun and slowly warm the planet, just like a blanket traps your body heat and keeps you cozy.

SHOP TILL YOU DROP

Toward the end of the Industrial Revolution, department stores started opening and clothing companies started advertising their exciting new fashions. Several fashion magazines hit the presses for the first time in the 1870s, and department stores held some of the first fashion shows ever in the early 1900s. Fashion was finally available to regular folks. People were excited to shop, and companies were keen to make money. To make sure people kept shopping, companies changed their styles every year. They made shirts in different colors, moved the pockets on jackets and changed skirt lengths. This made people think last year's looks were out of style.

Long before photography became popular, the world's first fashion magazines, like this one from 1878, featured illustrations of the latest looks.
HULTON ARCHIVE/GETTY IMAGES

For many people, shopping is a hobby and the mall is a meeting place. I think it's more fun to play at the park!
CANADAPANDA/SHUTTERSTOCK.COM

Companies also used advertisements to try to convince people that buying new clothes would get them the things they really wanted in life, like fun times with friends and family. This was the beginning of **consumerism**, which involves continually buying things to satisfy our desires and find happiness. However, researchers have found that the more focused we are on collecting possessions like clothing, the less happy we actually are. Still, people are shopping more than ever today. Some even line up overnight for sales in order to get first dibs on the best deals. Modern malls, which started opening in the 1950s, are now popular places to hang out, and shopping is a hobby for many people.

GOING GLOBAL

One day my kids and I each randomly chose 10 items of clothing from our closets and looked at the labels to see where they were made. Our clothes came from 15 countries. This is because **globalization** makes it possible for fashion companies to do business around the world. In the 1990s, governments introduced **free trade agreements** that made it easier for countries to trade goods and services. American fashion companies like the Gap and Nike started **outsourcing** production to developing countries like China and India, where people are paid lower wages and materials are less expensive.

Companies started searching for the best deals on everything from cotton and zippers to dying and sewing. This led to complicated **supply chains**—the paths clothes take from producers to consumers. The material for your shirt could be grown in one country, woven in another and sewn in yet another!

Since companies could get clothes made for less money, they could sell them for less too. This led to an explosion in the number of discount retailers like Target, Old Navy and Walmart. Since then cheap clothes have been extremely popular, especially

The labels on your clothes can tell you all kinds of things, including what they're made of and where they were made.
ULAMONGE/GETTY IMAGES

among parents who don't want to spend a lot of money on outfits their kids will quickly outgrow or destroy on the playground.

Today less than 4 percent of clothes and shoes sold in the United States are made in the country. While the cost of just about everything else has gone up over the decades—ice cream, skating lessons, houses—we spend less on clothing than ever before. In the 1960s some basic kids' dresses cost the equivalent of $100 today. Similar dresses today cost about $20. And when things are cheap, people often buy more of them. In 2020 Americans bought an average of 52 garments and 6 pairs of shoes per person. That's a new piece of clothing every week!

In theory globalization is a win-win. Factories bring money into developing countries, which can help reduce poverty. They also provide jobs for people who may otherwise be unemployed. In exchange, people in developed countries get cheaper goods. But it isn't always a fair trade.

If you buy a new piece of clothing every week, like the average American does, your closet could quickly overflow.
SMIRART/SHUTTERSTOCK.COM

Discount retailers like Walmart can sell kids' raincoats for the same price as a pizza because they're made overseas, where labor and materials are cheap.
TIM BOYLE/GETTY IMAGES

Super-stylin' kids strut the runway at a fashion show.
GUPPYSS/SHUTTERSTOCK.COM

ONE CLICK AWAY

Have you ever shopped online for fashion? Online shopping started taking off in the 1990s, and now in the United States about 30 percent of fashion items are bought on the internet. While it's comfortable and convenient to shop from your couch, it comes at a cost.

If you shop online, companies can gather all kinds of information about you and use it to sell you more stuff.
SNEKSY/GETTY IMAGES

People often buy more when they shop online. Companies can collect a lot of ***data*** on you from the products you view, what you buy and what personal information you share. They can then use this information for ***targeted advertising***. If you look at a jacket on a retailer's website but don't buy it, an ad for that same jacket may show up on other websites you visit. If you're about to buy a new shirt, the store may suggest you get a scarf to match. Some online retailers offer free delivery if you spend over a certain amount, which encourages you to buy extra items to reach the limit. You can even get a clothing subscription, which is like a magazine subscription, and have a box of new outfits delivered to your door every month or season. Online shopping has become so popular that thousands of retail stores are closing every year. When stores were forced to shut their doors during the COVID-19 pandemic, there was a spike in the number of people shopping online and in the number of stores permanently closing.

Social media has also had a huge influence on how we shop and what we buy. Celebrities and fashion influencers are paid by brands to wear their products and post photos of themselves on sites like Facebook and Instagram. Influencers are stylish people with lots of followers and the ability to influence what other people buy. There are even kid influencers with millions of followers! Their parents are often behind their accounts, dressing them in trendy outfits, taking their photos and posting those images online. Celebrities and influencers seem to wear something new every day, making their fans think they should have huge wardrobes too.

TODAY'S TRENDS ARE TOMORROW'S TRASH

Dressing like a celebrity every day is now affordable for many people. In the 1990s and 2000s, *fast fashion* spread across the world and changed the way we shop. Fast fashion is like fast food. It's cheap, made quickly with low-quality ingredients and sold in international chains. It's also trendy and designed to make the latest looks available to all. To make clothing so fast, companies often copy ideas from other designers and pressure factories owners to work as quickly as possible. Some of the biggest fast-fashion brands are Zara, H&M and Forever 21, and they all make kids' clothes. Do you have any fast fashion in your closet?

Before fast fashion, most brands released two collections of clothing a year, spring/summer and fall/winter. Some fast-fashion retailers release new collections every week! They do this to get you to shop all the time to keep up with the latest trends. Fast fashion often falls apart after a few washes because it's so poorly made. Many people don't bother repairing their clothes because it costs so little to buy new items, and the old ones are already out of style. Fast fashion has turned clothing into a *disposable good*.

But how do fast-fashion companies make money when they're selling shirts for $5 and pants for $10? By selling lots and lots of them. Fast fashion is cheap, but it comes at a huge cost to people, animals and the planet.

A display at an H&M store in London, UK, promises new arrivals every day.
PCRUCIATTI/SHUTTERSTOCK.COM

Fashion Fact
Annual clothing production doubled from 2000 to 2014. More than 100 billion items of clothing were made in 2014.

CHAPTER TWO

Fashion's Footprint

TREE-SHIRTS AND PLASTIC PANTS

All of our clothes come from plants, animals, chemicals or a mixture of these materials. No matter what your shirt is made out of, producing it had an impact on the environment. Cotton is the most popular natural fabric in our closets. A lot of water, **pesticides** and chemical **fertilizers** are used to help cotton plants grow. Many chemicals in pesticides and fertilizers are toxic to people and the environment. In 2007 researchers working for Levi's discovered that it took about 400 gallons (1,500 liters) of water to grow the cotton needed for a single pair of the company's jeans. That's about enough water for you to drink for 1,000 days! (The company has since worked to reduce its water footprint.) A lot of this water comes from rivers and lakes. Cotton production has even made Central Asia's Aral Sea, a lake the size of Ireland, nearly disappear because farmers sucked up all the water from the rivers that feed it. Organic cotton is grown with much less water and without pesticides and chemical fertilizers.

Bales of cotton can be full of chemicals that may poison workers and people who live nearby.
CALEB HOLDER/SHUTTERSTOCK.COM

The Aral Sea in Kazakhstan and Uzbekistan was once home to tens of thousands of fish. Now it's a ship graveyard.
TRAFFIC_ANALYZER/GETTY IMAGES

Animals such as critically endangered Sumatran tigers can lose their homes when trees are cut down to make clothes.

SLOWMOTIONGLI/SHUTTERSTOCK.COM

We know plastic bottles are bad for the environment. But did you know that more than half of our clothes are made out of the same material as plastic bottles? *Synthetic* fabrics like polyester, nylon and spandex are actually plastic. They're made from *petroleum*, a substance that's found underground and is also used to make gasoline to fuel our cars. Getting petroleum out of the ground and turning it into fabric requires a lot of energy and creates a lot of pollution.

If you've ever hugged a tree, you may be surprised to hear that the rough trunk can be turned into smooth fabric called rayon. Every year more than 200 million trees are chopped down to make clothes. If those trees were placed end to end, they would circle the planet seven times! Some of these trees come from ancient and endangered forests in Canada, Indonesia and the Amazon. These forests are often in the territories of Indigenous Peoples who didn't give companies permission to cut them down. The ecosystems are also home to animals that are at risk of becoming extinct. Forests are the lungs of the planet: they inhale carbon dioxide and exhale oxygen, allowing us to breathe fresh air. A lot of chemicals are needed to turn trees into fabric, and the process wastes 70 percent of the tree.

If you play sports, you probably have some plastic in your closet. Soccer jerseys, dance leotards and hockey pants are all made from synthetic fabrics.

JOHN GIUSTINA/GETTY IMAGES

Every year in India, millions of Hindu pilgrims take a holy dip in the Ganges River to cleanse their souls. The river is one of the most polluted in the world thanks to all the leather tanneries dumping toxic waste into it.

ALISON WRIGHT/GETTY IMAGES

Fashion Fact

The fashion industry is one of the world's biggest consumers and polluters of water.

People in China say you can predict the "it" color of the season by looking at the color of the rivers because so much dye has been dumped in them.

RIVERBLUE

TOXIC THREADS

Have you ever wondered how your jeans got their blue color and worn-out look? Thousands of chemicals are used to bleach, dye, distress and soften materials. Chemicals can also make our clothes resistant to water, wrinkles, stains and even fire. Some chemicals are harmless, but others are hazardous to the environment and human health. Some toxic chemicals have been banned in developed countries but are still being used in developing countries, which is where most of our clothes are made. Exposure to these chemicals has been linked to cancer, skin problems and *developmental delays* among children. People who work with the chemicals or live around the factories are at the highest risk of harm, but traces of chemicals can remain on the clothes we buy.

After factory workers have used these chemicals, they often dump the toxic *wastewater* into rivers. This can poison wildlife and people. Many people rely on rivers for drinking water, growing crops, preparing food, washing clothes and cleaning their bodies. People continue to use the rivers because they have no other options or don't know how dangerous the water is. Some countries have laws against dumping, but they're often not enforced. Luckily rivers can recover, and there are projects underway to clean up some of them.

To give jeans the distressed look, factory workers sometimes use a technique called sandblasting, which involves spraying sand out of an air gun onto denim. The process releases dust that can cause a deadly lung disease if workers breathe it in. Fortunately an organization called the Clean Clothes Campaign has convinced more than 40 brands to stop sandblasting jeans.

DUMPING GROUNDS

Have you ever thrown out a sock with holes in the toes? All our old socks add up to a big problem. Every second a garbage truck's worth of textiles is dumped in a landfill or burned. Natural fibers are biodegradable, but synthetic fibers are not. When natural fibers break down, they release greenhouse gases. When synthetic fibers sit in the landfill, they release harmful chemicals into the environment.

Some clothes in the landfill are worn out, but others are brand-new. People toss their clothes in the garbage because it's convenient and they don't know what else to do with them. (Don't worry—I have some ideas for you in chapter 4.) More than half of fast-fashion items are thrown out within a year of being bought. Companies sometimes intentionally damage and dump the clothes they can't sell because they have nowhere to store them, they don't want to cheapen their brand by giving them away and it's less expensive than recycling them. Some retailers also throw away returned clothes because it's too much work to restock them, they're damaged or they're no longer in season. This is starting to change as people become more aware of the problem and demand that companies do better. In 2020 France became the first country to make it illegal for brands and retailers to destroy unsold or returned clothing.

Even the clothes we donate to thrift stores can end up in landfills, sometimes on the other side of the world. Thrift stores sell only a fraction of donations. The leftovers get recycled or sold overseas, mainly to Africa, where clothing dealers try to sell them. A lot of the clothes are of poor quality or damaged, so they go straight to the landfill. This steady stream of secondhand clothing also takes business away from local textile and clothing

A man sandblasts jeans to give them the distressed look. This is a dangerous technique that dozens of brands have banned.
ALLISON JOYCE

When people throw clothing in the garbage, it ends up in the landfill, where it can take anywhere from a couple of weeks to hundreds of years to decompose, depending on the material.
SRDJANNS74/GETTY IMAGES

makers because they can't compete with the prices and selection. As a result, several African countries, such as Uganda and Kenya, have banned secondhand clothing imports.

DIRTY LAUNDRY

The average American family does about 300 loads of laundry every year, using massive amounts of energy and water. Every time we wash synthetic fabrics, they shed super-small pieces of plastic called **microfibers** that flow down the drain and into rivers, lakes and oceans. Doing laundry releases about half a million tons of microfibers into the ocean every year. That's equivalent to more than 50 billion plastic bottles and weighs as much as 5,000 blue whales! Fish may eat the microfibers, and then people may eat the fish. Yoga pants for dinner, anyone?

Dry cleaning, which involves cleaning delicate clothes with chemicals in a special facility, can also be dangerous. Some of the chemicals are toxic and can harm the environment and the health of workers and those who live nearby. The chemicals can also stay on our "clean" clothes, making us sick too. Thankfully there are some eco-friendly alternatives, but they're often more expensive.

One cool new trend is washing your jeans only a few times a year, which saves water, energy and money.
BOWONPAT SAKAEW / EYEEM/GETTY IMAGES

Hanging your clothes out to dry makes them last longer and gives them a fresh scent.
MOHAMED IBRAHIM / EYEEM/GETTY IMAGES

HOT FASHION

Did you know the fashion industry is a major contributor to human-caused climate change? Producing clothes, packaging them and shipping them all over the world uses a ton of energy and produces a ton of pollution. Climate change is causing extreme weather, killing off species of plants and animals, damaging food and water systems and making people sick. Poor people in developing countries, many of whom make our clothes, are most vulnerable to climate change. When there's a heat wave in Boston, the air-conditioning goes on in the malls. When there's one in Bangladesh, people working in clothing factories suffer heatstroke.

Fashion Fact
The fashion industry is responsible for about 10 percent of greenhouse gas emissions. That's more than the emissions of all the airplanes and ships in the world!

LABOR BEHIND THE LABEL

When you get dressed in the morning, do you ever wonder who made your clothes and what their lives are like? Most pieces of clothing we own were touched by the hands of many workers, from the people who picked the cotton to the people who sewed on the tags. Some are treated well, but many are not.

Sweatshops are common in the garment industry today just as they were during the Industrial Revolution. Most of them are in developing countries, but there are also some in developed countries. Every day millions of people are forced to work long hours for low pay in terrible conditions. They don't earn enough money to pay for basic human needs like food, shelter and even clothing. The majority of garment workers are young women, and many have children. Sometimes they bring their kids to work or send them to live with relatives because they can't afford childcare. The factories are often cramped, hot, loud, dirty and unsafe, and workers are sometimes denied clean drinking water and bathroom breaks.

Cotton farmers in India hold up signs as part of a campaign launched by the organization Fashion Revolution to help people better understand where their clothes come from and who's involved in making them.
DEVINA SINGH/FAIRTRADE INDIA

In 2013 more than 1,100 people were killed and another 2,500 were injured when the Rana Plaza clothing factory in Bangladesh collapsed. The day before, people had found deep cracks in the walls of the eight-story building—a sign that it was unsafe. Managers forced their employees to work anyway. Workers were making clothing for brands like Zara, Walmart, Joe Fresh and the Children's Place, and were under pressure to meet deadlines. It was the deadliest garment-factory disaster ever, but sadly there have since been many more.

Why are garment workers treated so poorly? Brands typically don't own the factories or take responsibility for the conditions. They usually want to produce clothing at the lowest cost possible so they can keep selling cheap clothes and making money. Factories are competing with each other for business from the brands, so they may cut corners to keep costs down. Governments also want business from the brands because it brings money into their countries. When workers try to form or join unions, they are often fired, attacked or even arrested.

The 2013 Rana Plaza collapse in Bangladesh put a spotlight on the dangerous working conditions faced by the people who make our clothes. BAYAZID AKTER/DREAMSTIME.COM

KIDS AT WORK

Picture yourself spending your days sewing sequins on shirts instead of going to school wearing one of those shirts. Child labor is against the law in most countries, but children continue to work in the poorest parts of the world, including areas of China, India and Thailand. About 152 million children are doing jobs that are harmful to their health and development and interfere with their education. Some children are slaves, meaning they're forced to work and aren't paid. Many children, even kindergarten-aged kids, work in the fashion industry.

Kids are often given jobs that take advantage of their small fingers, like picking cotton, sewing on buttons and trimming threads. Some children even move away from their families to go to work. Factory bosses sometimes trick poor parents by

A young boy works at a clothing factory in Bangladesh. KRUIT/SHUTTERSTOCK.COM

promising their children well-paying jobs, comfortable accommodations and opportunities to go to school. In reality the conditions are awful. The number of child laborers is slowly going down, thanks to the efforts of governments and nonprofit organizations like Fair Wear Foundation, which has convinced more than 130 brands to sign a code of labor practices that includes not using child labor. Today about one in 10 children in the world is working rather than learning, playing and spending time with friends and family. Would you buy a shirt if you knew a kid your age had made it?

DRESSED TO KILL

Millions of animals are injured or killed for fashion every year. Some are raised on farms and others are caught in the wild. Their skins become sneakers, their wool becomes sweaters and their feathers become stuffing in winter coats. Some people think we shouldn't wear animal products at all. Others think it's okay as long as the animals aren't endangered or mistreated. What do you think?

Most fur and leather come from developing countries that don't have or follow animal welfare laws. Animals often live in dirty, cramped conditions and are killed in cruel ways. Those that are shorn for their wool or plucked for their feathers may also suffer, and the mistreatment isn't only happening in developing countries. An investigation by People for the Ethical Treatment of Animals (PETA) found that sheep in Australia and the United States are regularly abused.

Indigenous Peoples have always hunted animals for clothing, food and other products. For example, Inuit hunt adult seals, then turn their skins into warm, waterproof clothing and eat their meat. They also sell sealskins. However, animal-rights groups have been trying to stop the seal hunt since the 1960s by using images of adorable harp seal pups with fluffy white fur,

Inuit have long hunted adult seals to feed and clothe their families and make money by selling sealskins. But in the 1960s, animal-rights activists started using images of baby harp seals to turn people against sealskin.
TOP: GALAXIID/ALAMY STOCK PHOTO
BOTTOM: VLADIMIR MELNIK/SHUTTERSTOCK.COM

known as whitecoats. In the 1980s, Canada banned the killing of whitecoats and the European Union banned products made from whitecoats. While this has saved the lives of millions of seals, it has harmed the livelihoods of thousands of Inuit hunters. Even though Inuit don't traditionally hunt whitecoats, all sealskins got a bad reputation, and people stopped buying them.

COPYCATS

We all know it's wrong to copy someone else's work, but fast-fashion companies steal ideas all the time. When they do this, they're profiting from someone else's work and creativity and often taking business away from the original creator. Copycats get away with it because fashion is not fully protected by copyright laws in some countries, including Canada and the United States.

Fashion companies also steal from cultures. ***Cultural appropriation*** involves using traditional knowledge, methods and designs from cultural groups without permission and in ways that ignore their significance or sacredness. For example, many companies have recreated Indigenous headdresses and sold them to non-Indigenous people as fashion accessories. This is offensive because in Indigenous communities, such as the Sioux tribes, headdresses are culturally, spiritually and politically significant, and only designated people can wear them. Due to Indigenous people speaking out against cultural appropriation, several music festivals have banned headdresses.

Indigenous headdresses, such as the one worn here by Chief Arvol Looking Horse of the Lakota Sioux Nation, symbolize strength and bravery and should only be worn by certain people. But several fast-fashion retailers have sold knockoff headdresses, which is very disrespectful to Indigenous Peoples.
ANGUS MORDANT

PINK IS FOR GIRLS AND BLUE IS FOR BOYS?

Think about the differences you've noticed between clothes that are designed for girls and clothes that are designed for boys. Girls' clothes are often pink, flimsy and covered in cupcakes, rainbows and unicorns. Boys' clothes are often blue, durable and feature sports, video games and dinosaurs. Boys' shirts have messages like *Be a hero* and *Pure genius*. Girls' shirts say things like *I need a hero* and *I'm too pretty to do homework so my brother has to do it for me.*

Clothing companies are **gender stereotyping** when they make assumptions about your interests, abilities and aspirations based on your gender. This can sometimes discourage you from doing things that don't fit with stereotypical ideas of what boys and girls should do. If you're a girl and you see footballs only on boys' clothes, or if you're a boy and you see figure skates only on girls' clothes, what are you going to think? If you don't identify as a girl or a boy, you may feel like there are no clothes for you. On the positive side, several brands have created **unisex** lines of clothing, removed "boys" and "girls" labeling from clothing and eliminated gendered sections in stores. California is even considering making it law for large department stores to have a gender-neutral section.

Wearing clothes with positive messages can inspire you and everyone around you.
ANNIE OTZEN/GETTY IMAGES

MIRROR, MIRROR, ON THE WALL

Have you noticed that the vast majority of children in clothing advertisements are white and thin and don't have any physical or mental differences? The children on your school playground probably look a lot different. Our communities are full of people of different shapes, sizes, colors and abilities, but we don't always see that diversity reflected in the pages of fashion magazines. When fashion companies only use thin, white models, they're telling us that looking like that is "normal" and everyone else is "different." The fashion industry also promotes unrealistic beauty expectations.

Fortunately racial diversity is steadily increasing in fashion advertising campaigns, but it's still rare to see models with bigger bodies or with physical or mental differences. Several countries, including France, Italy and Israel, have banned underweight models to reduce the risk of models and members of the public developing low self-esteem and unhealthy habits.

It's rare to see models with physical and mental differences. Canadian ethical clothing company Little & Lively decided to change that by featuring this little girl, who has a rare genetic condition, in an advertising campaign.
TAYLOR REIGN PHOTOGRAPHY

CHAPTER THREE

Taking Action on Fashion

WHO MADE MY CLOTHES?

KEEP ON ASKING ???

STOP FAST FASHION

NOT BUYING IT

FEATUREFLASH PHOTO AGENCY/SHUTTERSTOCK.COM

TRENDSETTER

After years of being bullied for her dark skin, Kheris Rogers decided to launch her own clothing line in 2017, when she was 10 years old. She called it Flexin' In My Complexion, and her goal was to help other People of Color feel less alone and more confident in their skin. The Los Angeles girl started by printing *Flexin' In My Complexion* on T-shirts, which quickly sold out. She soon expanded her collection, and celebrities started wearing her clothing. The same year she launched her line, she became the youngest person ever to show her clothing at New York Fashion Week. Since then she's appeared on *America's Next Top Model*, guest starred as herself in a Nickelodeon miniseries called *Middle School Moguls*, launched a hair-product line and started a foundation to help kids in need.

PUTTING ON THE PRESSURE

Around the world, dozens of nonprofit organizations are working hard to make the fashion industry more ethical. They investigate issues, go on super-spy missions, meet with companies and governments, organize protests and try to get people to pay attention to the problems and the solutions. Here are just a few of the organizations doing good work.

Greenpeace pressures companies to stop using hazardous chemicals to make clothing. In 2011 Greenpeace investigators tested the wastewater of two large textile factories in China and found a wide range of hazardous chemicals. They figured out which fashion companies were using those factories, told them what they had discovered and asked them to stop using the chemicals. Some quickly agreed, while others needed some convincing. Greenpeace *activists* and regular people like you protested outside stores around the world to put pressure on brands. Eventually 80 companies, including H&M, Adidas and Levi's, agreed to stop using the chemicals by 2020 and have all made progress toward that goal.

Fashion Revolution educates people about the issues in the fashion industry and brings them together to take action. It also encourages the industry and governments to make positive changes. During Fashion Revolution Week the organization encourages people to ask brands, "Who made my clothes?"

Would someone wearing a sheep mask or a dress made out of used clothing get your attention? Activists from several organizations have staged protests outside clothing stores to bring attention to issues in the fashion industry.

INSET: COURTESY OF PEOPLE FOR THE ETHICAL TREATMENT OF ANIMALS (PETA); MAIN: ©BENTE STACHOWSKE/GREENPEACE

Clean Clothes Campaign improves working conditions for garment workers. It pressures governments and companies to make positive changes and helps workers fight for their rights. The organization was responsible for creating a workplace-safety agreement that was signed by more than 200 brands and made factories safer for over two million workers in Bangladesh.

Canopy works with brands and rayon producers to help them stop turning ancient and endangered forests into fabrics. So far more than 400 brands, including Gap, H&M and Zara, and producers representing more than 90 percent of the rayon production in the world have made this commitment.

People for the Ethical Treatment of Animals (PETA) leads attention-grabbing campaigns to get brands to stop using animal products. PETA investigators go undercover to expose animal abuse and then confront companies with the evidence and demand changes. They also ask people to *boycott* brands by not buying their products until the companies change. PETA has convinced hundreds of designers to stop using fur and even got a high school in Los Angeles to change its uniform requirements so students don't have to wear leather belts.

Let Clothes Be Clothes fights gender stereotyping in the design and marketing of children's clothing. It raises awareness of the issue, challenges irresponsible retailers and supports unisex retailers.

Most of these organizations welcome volunteers, including kids, so there are lots of opportunities to get involved in causes you care about.

A Greenpeace activist dressed as a mannequin warns shoppers that hazardous chemicals have been found in Zara clothing.

©JONAS GRATZER/GREENPEACE

29

Ecolabels can help you find ethical clothing.

NOT BUYING IT

Individuals also take action when they see brands behaving badly. Sometimes people go to the media, start petitions on websites like Change.org or post about the issues on social media using the **hashtag** #NotBuyingIt. If there's enough backlash, the company may change its practices and apologize. That's what happened when I wrote an article for the *Huffington Post* about sexist firefighter and police-officer Halloween costumes that were being sold at Value Village in 2014 and asked the thrift-store chain to stop selling them. The boys' costumes looked like the real uniforms, while the girls' costumes were short, skimpy, skin-tight dresses. When the article went viral, Value Village apologized and stopped selling the costumes. Victory!

PUT A LABEL ON IT

Have you ever noticed labels on your food telling you that it's organic, fair trade or vegan? They're called ecolabels, and they exist for fashion too. Organizations create ecolabels to make it easier for you to make ethical choices. Fashion brands earn these ecolabels by meeting certain criteria, just like you get badges for passing levels in swimming lessons.

Fashion ecolabels can tell you if your clothes are organic, fair trade, made from recycled materials or free of dangerous chemicals. They can also assure you that the people and animals involved in making your clothes were treated with respect and that making your clothes didn't contribute to climate change. See if you can spot some ecolabels next time you're shopping.

Be careful of companies that claim their products are "ethical," "green" or "eco-friendly" without reputable ecolabels backing them up. They may be greenwashing, which means making misleading claims about how environmentally friendly a product is.

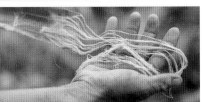

Innovative company Ananas Anam turns pineapple leaves that would have otherwise been wasted into a sustainable material called Piñatex, which is then used to make all kinds of fashion items, from shoes to hats.

ANANAS ANAM

FRESH FABRICS

One day you'll be able to wear a fruit salad to school. Companies are already making fabrics from banana stems, coconut husks and orange peels. They're also making leather alternatives from apple peels, grape skins and pineapple leaves. These materials are eco-friendly and use parts of the fruits that may otherwise be wasted.

Companies are also hard at work in the lab trying to grow leather and fur without animals, and heading to the ocean in search of solutions. They're turning seaweed and ocean plastics into fabrics and using a fiber from shrimp shells to help bind dyes to fabrics and reduce the need for chemicals. Shoes and clothes are also being made from the billions of plastic bottles that are thrown out every year. But the most impressive new material has to be carbon dioxide emissions. A company called 10XBeta made a pair of shoes out of the greenhouse gas as part of a competition. The designers captured carbon dioxide, added a **catalyst** and created the first shoe without a carbon footprint!

In addition to all these cool new materials, brands are also using more sustainable traditional fabrics like organic cotton, linen and hemp. Natural dyes from plants are also making a comeback from ancient times.

This Timberland sneaker was made out of six plastic bottles.

JO GALVAO/SHUTTERSTOCK.COM

No sheep were hurt in the making of these pj's! Wee Woollies makes its children's clothing and sleepwear out of sustainable, ethical merino wool from New Zealand.
CINDY FINLEY/EMILY HULL

ETHICAL BRANDS TO THE RESCUE

There are lots of ethical brands leading the fashion revolution. They're using eco-friendly materials. They're making sure everyone in their supply chains is treated with respect. They're challenging gender stereotypes and traditional ideas of beauty. And they're giving back to the community. Here are just a few companies that are making kids' fashion with a conscience.

Wee Woollies makes all of its clothing and sleepwear with wool from healthy merino sheep in New Zealand. The sheep get to roam freely and never get buzzcuts that leave them shivering. Wee Woollies also uses nontoxic dyes, and all items are sewn in Vancouver, British Columbia, where workers are paid and treated well. The wool is certified ethical by two organizations, guaranteeing the sheep are well cared for and the fabric is sustainable. Everything is gender-neutral, and you can buy patches made from leftover fabric to repair any holes.

Smoking Lily designs, sews and prints all its clothes in its studio in Victoria, British Columbia. The brand uses ethical materials from Canadian suppliers such as nontoxic inks and OEKO-TEX-certified fabrics. OEKO-TEX is an ecolabel that guarantees certified clothing is free from harmful substances. Smoking Lily finds creative ways to use every single scrap of fabric so it doesn't produce any waste. In fact, all the kids' clothing and accessories like scrunchies and headbands are made from leftover bits of fabric from adult items. In 2020 Smoking Lily launched a take-back program called Reloved. Customers brought in their old items for the staff to repair or redesign and then resell, with the profits going to a local charity.

Smoking Lily sometimes opens its studio to the public so people can learn how its clothes are made. RAINA DELISLE

Smoking Lily uses scraps of fabric to make onesies and other kids' clothing. RAINA DELISLE

Patagonia uses ethical materials like organic cotton, recycled polyester, nontoxic dyes and humane animal products. The outdoor-wear brand ensures all workers in its supply chain are paid a living wage and treated well. It encourages people to trade in their used gear for store credit and resells it through an online secondhand shop called Worn Wear. Used items that are too worn out to be resold are upcycled into new items. It also gives 1 percent of its sales to 1% for the Planet, which funds environmental organizations.

Not only does Princess Awesome and Boy Wonder challenge gender stereotypes, it also features diverse models and makes matching kid and adult outfits.
KATIE JETT WALLS PHOTOGRAPHY

TOMS gives back in a big way. For every pair of shoes you buy, the company gives a pair to a child in need. When you buy sunglasses, someone gets an eye exam, prescription glasses or sight-saving surgery. And if you purchase a bag, TOMS provides a safe-birth kit for a pregnant woman. The company also uses sustainable materials and closely monitors its supply chain.

Princess Awesome and Boy Wonder smashes gender stereotypes with cool clothes that accurately reflect the diverse interests of boys and girls. There are boys' clothes with unicorns and rainbows and girls' clothes with dragons and trains. The clothes are made in certified ethical factories in the United States and abroad. One factory in Chicago even closes at 3:00 p.m. so the workers can pick their kids up from school.

RENT YOUR NEXT LOOK

Have you ever had to buy a new outfit for a special occasion, like a wedding or graduation, and then never worn it again? Me too! The good news is you may never have to do that again. Several clothing-rental businesses have opened in recent years, and many of them offer outfits for kids. Most companies operate online, but there may be a local rental shop in your area. To rent from an online company, you select an outfit from their website and it's delivered right to your doorstep. After you wear it, you send it back. You don't even have to wash it!

Renting saves you money, and it saves the environment by reducing the number of clothes that are produced. However, shipping clothes all over the place, cleaning them after every use and packaging them over and over again causes a lot of pollution and waste. Some companies use eco-friendly cleaning products and recyclable packaging to reduce their impact.

Clothing rentals make it possible to dress like a princess for the day. Companies like Rainey's Closet, where these outfits are from, even offer party rentals so you and your friends can celebrate in style.
NICHOLE LEE PHOTOGRAPHY

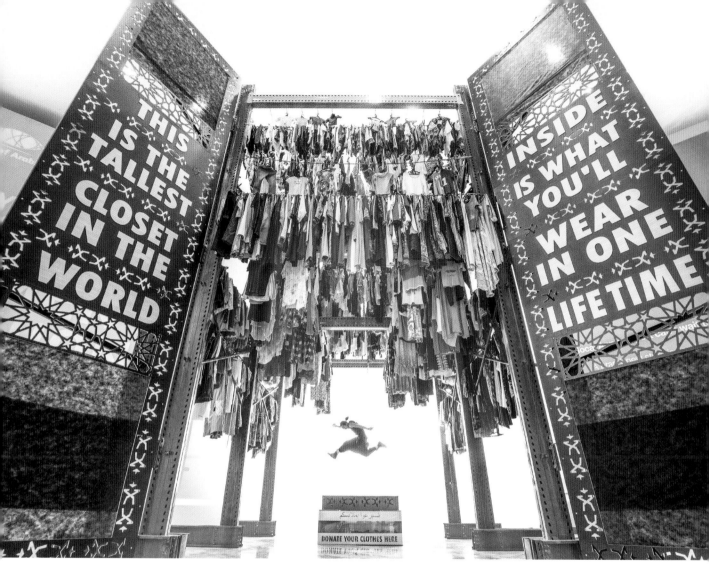

A team of artists, designers and volunteers built an art installation called the World's Tallest Closet and hung 3,000 pieces of clothing in it to show how many items a person may go through in a lifetime.

WORLD'S TALLEST CLOSET/BENJAMIN VON WONG/VONWONG.COM

Fashion Fact

The amount of clothing and shoes going to the dump in the United States has more than doubled since 2000. More than 9 million tons were thrown out in 2018. That's equivalent to about 55 pounds (25 kilograms) per person!

SECONDHAND SHOPPING GOES ONLINE

Is that outfit you only wore once still hanging in the back of your closet? Secondhand shops that sell your clothes for you have been around for a long time, but now there are several online retailers doing the same thing. Two of the biggest ones are thredUP and the RealReal, and they both sell kids' fashion. You can send in or drop off your clothes, and the shop selects the items it can sell, posts them on its website and ships them to the buyer. You get a percentage of the sale price, and anything that can't be sold is recycled, donated or returned to you.

Some brands have started their own resale shops. For example, you can bring in your used North Face gear and the company will give you store credit, clean and refurbish your items and sell them through its online Renewed shop.

Websites that allow you to sell all kinds of items directly to other people, like eBay and Etsy, have also been around for a long time, but there are now sites specializing in fashion. Poshmark is one of the most popular sites, and it sells kids' fashion. You take photos of your items, post them on the website and send them to the buyer.

EREK HANSEN

THE SECOND LIVES OF CLOTHES

You recycle your old schoolwork and your empty milk jugs, but worn-out clothes often end up in the trash. Many people don't know that clothes can be recycled too. More and more cities are starting textile recycling programs. Some collect clothing at the curb with your other recyclables, while others have bins or buildings where you can drop off items. A growing number of brands—including Zara, H&M and Forever 21—are collecting used clothing in stores so it can be recycled. Most of them accept clothing from any brand in any condition and give you a credit toward your next purchase—just be aware that this encourages you to do more shopping. Many thrift stores also accept recyclables.

Recycling companies sort clothes in warehouses. The items that are still wearable are usually shipped overseas. The rest are cut into rags for painters and mechanics, spun into yarn for new clothes or shredded into stuffing for things like furniture, carpet padding and car seats. The rubber from old shoes can be used to make new ones or squishy playground and track surfaces.

TRENDSETTER

When Erek Hansen was nine years old, he read an article about an organization that recycles denim into home insulation for people in need, such as those rebuilding after a hurricane. Erek held a denim drive in his driveway and worked with a local business, collecting 1,684 pieces of denim. More than a decade later, he continues to hold annual drives for denim and shoes through his organization Go Green Ohio. The shoes are given to people in need or recycled. As of June 2020, Erek had collected 34,101 denim items and 19,395 pairs of shoes!

If you have to wear a mask to school, you may as well match it to your outfit!

HELENA LOPES/PEXELS.COM

PIVOTING DURING THE PANDEMIC

People in the fashion industry tend to be creative. When faced with challenges, they often come up with clever solutions. When there were shortages of protective gear during the COVID-19 pandemic in 2020, several clothing companies started making gowns and masks for healthcare workers. Fashion brands and hobby sewers, including lots of kids, also started making masks for the public in an array of colors and patterns, turning them into stylish accessories.

GOING HIGH TECH...AND LOW TECH

Would you buy a piece of clothing that doesn't exist in real life? Virtual clothing is an emerging trend that comes with social and environmental benefits. You can now buy a piece of digital clothing and have it virtually tailored onto a photo of yourself, similar to how you can buy outfits for your avatars in video games. Virtual clothing is ideal for influencers, who can avoid buying new items they only wear once, or for that special family photo. Some designers have even used virtual clothing in fashion shows by projecting holograms onto models.

Going low tech can also have benefits. In January 2020 *Italian Vogue* made a statement on sustainability by eliminating photos from the magazine. Instead the pages were filled with illustrations, just like magazines back in the 1870s. In a note to readers,

Putting together a fashion magazine has an impact on the environment. All those cameras and lights use a lot of energy!

LANE OATEY / BLUE JEAN IMAGES/GETTY IMAGES

the editor in chief outlined what it takes to fill one issue with photos, including 20 flights, 60 international deliveries, food waste from catering, plastic for wrapping the garments and electricity to recharge phones and cameras.

CELEBRATING SUSTAINABLE STYLE

In the summer of 2019, I went to a different kind of fashion show called VIM Future Oceans. The runway was the dock of the Victoria International Marina, and the clothes were made out of ocean plastics. The Ocean Legacy Foundation had collected the plastics during ocean cleanups, and the designers had picked through the piles to create their pieces. The results were impressive and inspiring, and got a lot of people talking about plastic pollution and ethical fashion. Similar events are happening all over the world. If you can't attend one in person, you can feel like you're there by watching YouTube shows about the Redress Design Award, the world's biggest sustainable-fashion-design competition.

Celebrities are also stepping up to celebrate ethical fashion. In 2010 ethical fashion consultant Livia Firth started the Green Carpet Challenge to encourage celebrities to wear sustainable styles on the red carpet. In 2021 singer-songwriter and animal-rights activist Billie Eilish wore an Oscar de la Renta dress to the Met Gala, a party that's like the fashion Olympics, on the condition that the designer stop using fur. Designers have also created green-carpet collections, and there are even Green Carpet Fashion Awards to celebrate ethical fashion leaders.

There are so many exciting new developments in ethical fashion that a museum opened to celebrate them. At the Fashion for Good Museum in Amsterdam, visitors learn about the history and future of ethical fashion and how they can take action. The museum offers virtual tours, so you and other visitors from around the world can be guided through the exhibits with an expert host from the comfort of your home.

Vancouver designer and third-grade teacher Kyle Nylund made this dress with his students and showed it at the VIM Future Oceans fashion show in 2019. They made the dress, modeled by artist Carling Jackson, out of ocean debris collected by the Ocean Legacy Foundation.
ZEV ABOSH/PHOTOART4U

CHAPTER FOUR

Be a Fashion Hero

REPAIR

REUSE

RENT

REDUCE

RECYCLE

REPURPOSE

RESEARCH

Looking for a fun rainy-day activity?
Try counting all the clothes in your closet
(or just hiding in it). According to one estimate,
most people wear only 20 percent of their
clothes on a regular basis.
KETUT SUBIYANTO/PEXELS

THE SEVEN Rs OF ETHICAL FASHION

You probably know the three Rs—reduce, reuse and recycle. When it comes to ethical fashion, there are four more—research, repurpose, repair and rent. If you follow the seven Rs, you'll be well on your way to becoming a fashion hero.

Reduce: Choose Quality over Quantity

Do you have any idea how many pieces of clothing you have? Go ahead and count. Don't forget what you're wearing, what's in your laundry hamper and what may be hiding under your bed. You can skip socks and underwear. My kids and I did this and were shocked by our totals. We had over 100 pieces each. The more clothing you buy, the bigger your fashion footprint.

After counting our clothes, my kids and I decided to downsize our wardrobes by participating in the Project 333 minimalist fashion challenge. Project 333 involves dressing in 33 items or fewer for three months and putting the rest of your clothing in boxes. (Socks, underwear, pajamas and sportswear don't count.) At the end of the challenge, my kids and I realized we only need 33 items of clothing. We had chosen our favorite pieces and felt

Learning how to make your own clothes is a great way to gain an appreciation for how much work goes into the process.
VGAJIC/GETTY IMAGES

we had enough variety in our wardrobes. Plus, it was a lot easier to decide what to wear in the morning! We gave away and sold most of the items in our boxes.

You can also try a fashion fast and not buy any clothes for a certain period of time. Extinction Rebellion, a global environmental movement, encourages people to boycott fashion for a year. Do you think you could do it?

When you do go shopping, you can look for high-quality items that will last a long time. The 30 Wears Challenge encourages people to only buy clothes they will wear at least 30 times. That means you have to like the items enough to wear them 30 times, and they have to withstand 30 wears and several washes without falling apart. You'll have to pay more for high-quality clothing, but you'll save money in the long run. Think of it this way: a $30 T-shirt you wear 30 times costs $1 per wear, and a $10 T-shirt you wear five times before it falls apart costs $2 per wear.

You can also reduce your fashion footprint by washing and drying your clothes less often and only when necessary. Just because you wore something all day doesn't mean it's dirty.

Before you get a new piece of clothing, ask yourself if you will wear it at least 30 times.
MIXETTO/GETTY IMAGES

Children refashion a brave volunteer's outfit in under an hour as part of Fashion Machine, *a live performance event produced by Theatre SKAM in Victoria, BC.*

PAMELA BETHEL/SKAM.CA/FASHION-MACHINE

Unless you did something like spill spaghetti on yourself or sweat on the soccer field, you may be able to wear your clothes again. The less laundry you do, the less water and energy you'll use and the longer your clothing will last. You'll also save time and money.

Reuse: If You Love It, Pass It On

When you counted your clothes, did you come across any hand-me-downs? People have been passing on clothing that's no longer their size or style to friends or family members for centuries. Hand-me-downs are particularly popular among children because you often outgrow your clothes long before you outwear them.

There are lots of other ways to find and share preloved fashion. My kids and I host and attend clothing exchanges, where people bring their old items and swap for new ones. We also donate clothes to organizations that give them directly to people in need, such as food banks, homeless shelters and single-parent resource centers. During the COVID-19 pandemic, we launched a project called the COVID-19 Closet Collaborative. We created a Facebook group and encouraged people to donate clothes and shoes they no longer wanted. We then collected the donations, washed them, posted photos of them on our group and asked if anyone wanted them. When people requested items, we delivered them. We redistributed hundreds of items in two months! (We did most of our collections and deliveries on our bikes, scooters or rollerblades to reduce our fashion footprint.)

My kids and a couple of friends check out the items available at a clothing exchange we hosted in a park.
RAINA DELISLE

We also shop, sell and donate at secondhand stores. Some thrift stores are operated by charities, and the money they make helps them run their programs. If you shop or donate at an SPCA thrift store, you're helping the organization take care of animals. Some charity thrift stores, like the Salvation Army, give vouchers to low-income families so they can shop for clothing for free.

Other thrift stores are for-profit businesses and make money when you shop or donate. Value Village, also known as Savers, is the largest for-profit thrift retailer in the world and relies on charities to fill the racks at its 330-plus stores. Charities collect donated goods and deliver them to Value Village, and people drop off donations in stores. Value Village pays charities between 4 and 44 cents per pound of clothing according to investigations into the company. If you donate a pair of jeans that weighs half a pound, the charities could get as little as two cents. Some people think Value Village is unethical because it pays charities so little while passing itself off as a charitable organization. At the same time, Value Village helps charities raise about $160 million and keeps 700 million pounds of reusable goods out of landfills every year.

Maybe you would like to make some money from selling your old clothes and save up for something special. Resale shops buy the clothing they think they can sell when you bring it in, and consignment shops pay you a percentage of the sale price if your items sell. You can also buy and sell clothes online, but you may need an adult to help you.

Recycle: Don't Throw Out that Solo Sock

In addition to recycling your worn-out clothes through a shop or your city's textile recycling program, you can also look for ways to recycle them yourself. You can ask local painters, mechanics, animal shelters and art schools if they want your old clothes for rags. You may be able to use your old clothes for craft projects. My family has made sock puppets out of solo socks, and pillows and blankets for dolls and stuffies out of old flannel shirts.

Before you donate your clothes to thrift stores, you may want to take some time to research them and make sure their business practices align with your values.
JGI/JAMIE GRILL/GETTY IMAGES

Research: Be a Fashion Detective

Research isn't just for school projects. You can also put your detective skills to work to find out if a clothing brand is ethical. A good place to start is on a company's website, where you may find information on their commitment to sustainability and social justice. If you don't find the answers you're looking for, you can send the company an email or fill out a feedback form on its website. Fashion Revolution has a form letter that you can send to brands from its website. You can also google the brand to see if there have been any negative news stories about it or if any advocacy organizations have raised any concerns about it.

There are also people and organizations that have done the research for you. DoneGood is a website that lists hundreds of ethical brands and allows you to search by the issues that matter most to you. And Good On You is a website and app that rates brands on how they treat people, animals and the planet.

When you're in a shop, you can ask the salespeople questions and look for ecolabels. The more information you have about clothes, the easier it is to make ethical choices.

You can find out all kinds of things about clothing companies by doing some research online. A mom-approved use of screen time!
FG TRADE/GETTY IMAGES

Young people participate in a march to raise awareness of the importance of ethical fashion.
FASHION REVOLUTION PHILIPPINES

Repurpose: Be a Fashion Magician

Have a pair of jeans with holes in the knees? Cut off the lower legs and turn them into shorts. Have a sweater with stains down the front? Cut off the arms and make a pair of arm warmers. There are endless ways to *refashion* clothing.

You can also use the fabric from old clothes to make something totally different. The jersey you wore when you won the championship can be transformed into a throw cushion, and the sweater your grandma knit can be given a second life as a stuffed animal. My kids and I used an old pair of jeans to jazz up the jars of homemade jam we gave as Christmas gifts one year. We used pinking shears to cut out squares of fabric, placed them over the lids of the jars and tied them with hemp string. They looked fabulous, and the jam was pretty tasty too. There's a large community of people who are passionate about repurposing, and you can find plenty of inspiration and tutorials online.

Repair: Make It New Again

Lots of people get rid of clothes because they have rips, holes, missing buttons or broken zippers. Most clothing can be repaired—you just need to know how to do it or find someone who does. You can take a sewing class or watch video tutorials online. If it's too hard to repair something on your own, you can take it to a tailor or a cobbler.

Rent: The Sisterhood (or Brotherhood) of Sharing Clothes

Have you read the book or seen the film *The Sisterhood of the Traveling Pants*? In the story four friends take turns wearing one pair of pants, despite their different body sizes. In addition to renting clothes from a growing number of businesses, you can also ask a friend if you can borrow an outfit and offer to lend items from your closet. It's a great way to try out different looks and make sure every piece of clothing gets at least 30 wears.

A boy gets a sewing lesson from his grandmother. What would you turn this floral fabric into?
MESQUITAFMS/GETTY IMAGES

These cute kitties used to be ugly sweaters! Designer mirabeans makes one-of-a-kind clothing and accessories for kids and adults out of upcycled sweaters and other reclaimed textiles. The kitties are made out of some of the smallest scraps.
ADOPT-A-KITTY UPCYCLED KITTENS BY MIRABEANS

Fashion Fact
If everyone bought one fashion item used rather than new this year, we would save 5.7 billion pounds of carbon dioxide emissions. That's equivalent to taking more than half a million cars off the road for a year!

SHOP LOCAL AND ETHICAL

Shopping local has many benefits. Local boutiques often have strong commitments to sustainability and the community. When you shop at a local retailer rather than a big chain store, more of your money stays in your community. Local businesses are much more likely than chains to work with other local businesses, such as accountants and printers, and support local charities, sports teams and schools. Local businesses also define the character of your community. Would you rather see five independent shops downtown or one giant Walmart?

Maker markets are also great places to find unique clothing items and meet the people who made them. You can hear the story behind the clothing and ask questions. You'll never have to ask, "Who made my clothes?" When you buy directly from the maker, you're reducing your environmental impact because the item doesn't have to travel far.

Want to create your own personal style and stand out from the crowd? Shop for clothes at local boutiques rather than fast-fashion outlets, and pick up some unique items.
ELVA ETIENNE/GETTY IMAGES

LOVE YOUR CLOTHING

It can be tough to avoid spilling soup on your sweater or sprinting outside in your socks when your friend shows up at your home, but taking proper care of your clothing can extend its life and reduce your fashion footprint. Think of your clothes as valuable personal possessions (which they are) and treat them gently. You shouldn't be afraid to have fun and get messy—just make sure you're wearing the right outfit for the activity.

MARK YOUR CALENDAR

You can celebrate ethical fashion and push for change in the fashion industry all year long. Several organizations have launched initiatives to bring us together and inspire us to become more conscious consumers.

Second Hand September: Forget hitting the mall for back-to-school clothes. Oxfam wants you to take a month off buying new clothes. Don't worry—you can still go *thrifting*.

Buy Nothing Day: Held on or around Black Friday, one of the busiest shopping days of the year, Buy Nothing Day is a worldwide protest against consumerism. Adbusters Media Foundation encourages you to take the day off shopping and organize or participate in a protest such as a zombie walk around the mall or a "whirly-mart," which involves getting a group of friends together and pushing empty shopping carts around a store in a conga line. Make sure to ask an adult for permission first!

Make Smthng Week: After a day of buying nothing, Greenpeace and other organizations encourage you to spend a week making something. Held around the same time as Buy Nothing Day, this week includes hundreds of events across dozens of countries.

Fashion Revolution Week: The week of April 24, the anniversary of the Rana Plaza building collapse, is a time to ask brands and producers about their supply chains. To do this, Fashion Revolution encourages you to take a selfie in a piece of clothing with the label showing while holding a poster that reads *Who made my clothes?*, post the photo on social media and tag the company. (You may need an adult to help you.) Some brands won't respond, but others may have the answers you're looking for.

National Thrift Shop Day: August 17 is a day to celebrate secondhand shopping. Some shops mark the occasion by holding special sales or events.

A man dressed as Santa Claus protests in one of the busiest shopping districts in the world, Oxford Street in London, UK, on Buy Nothing Day.
ADBUSTERS

My daughter learns how to turn flax into linen at Fibrations, an annual festival of fibers in Victoria, BC.
RAINA DELISLE

JOIN THE MOVEMENT!

What changes would you like to see in the fashion industry? Your voice matters, and you can use it to push for positive change. Write to companies and politicians and ask them to help make the fashion industry more fair, safe, clean and transparent. Sign online petitions started by organizations like Greenpeace and PETA demanding changes in the industry. Commit to wearing only ethical clothing, whether it's thrift-store finds, ethical designs or handmade items. Spread the word! When someone compliments your outfit, use it as an opportunity to tell them about your commitment to ethical fashion. You may inspire them to become a fashion hero too! Together we can help transform the fashion industry so we can look stylish without harming people, animals and the planet.

There are lots of easy things you can do to be a fashion hero, like committing to buying only ethical clothing.

TRENDSETTER

High school students often celebrate graduation with a formal dance called a prom. Getting dressed up in fancy clothes like gowns and tuxedos is a big part of the party. In 2015 Erinne Paisley decided to do something different. Instead of spending hundreds of dollars on an outfit she would probably wear just once, she made her own dress, using a pair of scissors, tape, ribbon and her old math homework. The teen from Victoria, British Columbia, also made herself into a walking billboard for an important cause she cares about—women's rights. On her dress she wrote in red ink, *I've received my education. Not every woman has that right. MALALA.org.* Erinne donated the money she would have spent on a prom dress to the Malala Fund and encouraged others to do the same. The Malala Fund is an organization dedicated to giving every girl in the world the opportunity to go to school. Erinne's story went viral, bringing awareness to ethical fashion and women's rights.

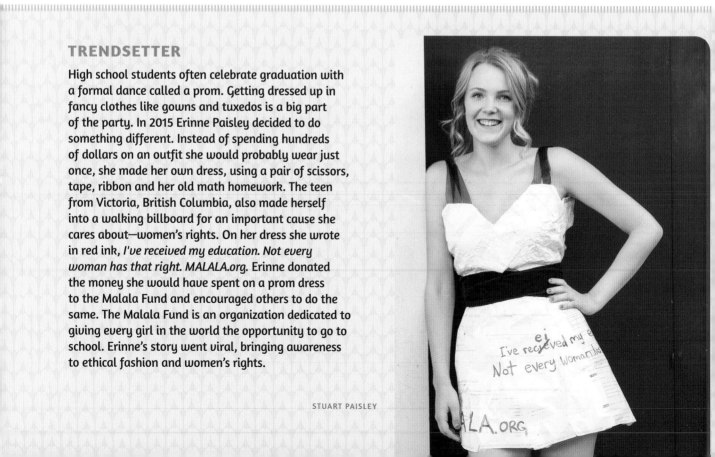

Acknowledgments

Expressing gratitude is always in style, so here we go! This book wouldn't have happened without my generous editor, Kirstie Hudson, who gifted me the idea and offered insightful feedback throughout the writing process. Thank you, Kirstie and the entire Orca team.

Thank you to my husband, Gabe, and daughters, Ocea and Elodie, for giving me the time, space, inspiration and encouragement to write this book. I appreciate all the young fashionistas and the baby fashionisto in my family—Mayabelle, Ocea, Elodie, Ophelia and Luke—for wearing, caring for and passing on the secondhand styles I've curated over the years. I'm grateful to my parents, Colleen and John Torsky, and my friends Heather Barnes and Nick Finley for taking care of Ocea and Elodie during crunch time. A special thanks to my mom for inspiring me to become an ethical fashionista by dressing me in thrift-store finds as a kid and giving me some groovy hand-me-downs from the 1970s, which I still wear today. I'll be forever thankful to all the people from companies, nonprofit organizations and research and educational institutions who shared their knowledge and stories with me. I also appreciate the photographers whose art brings these pages to life. Last but not least, a huge thank-you to all the people in the fashion industry who are committed to ethical fashion—your work is inspiring, and it's making a difference!

Resources

Print

Fyvie, Erica. *Trash Revolution: Breaking the Waste Cycle.* Toronto, ON: Kids Can Press, 2018.

Jones, Kari. *Ours to Share: Coexisting in a Crowded World.* Victoria, BC: Orca Book Publishers, 2019.

Mulder, Michelle. *Pocket Change: Pitching In for a Better World.* Victoria, BC: Orca Book Publishers, 2016.

Paisley, Erinne. *Can Your Outfit Change the World?* Victoria, BC: Orca Book Publishers, 2018.

Online

Canopy: canopyplanet.org

Clean Clothes Campaign: cleanclothes.org

DoneGood: donegood.co

Ecolabel Index: ecolabelindex.com

Extinction Rebellion: rebellion.global

Fair Wear Foundation: fairwear.org

Fashion for Good: fashionforgood.com

Fashion Revolution: fashionrevolution.org

Fashion Takes Action: fashiontakesaction.com

Global Organic Textile Standard: global-standard.org

Good On You: goodonyou.eco

Greenpeace, Detox My Fashion: greenpeace.org/international/act/detox

Kids for Saving Earth: kidsforsavingearth.org

Labour Behind the Label: labourbehindthelabel.org

Let Clothes Be Clothes: letclothesbeclothes.co.uk

Make Smthng Week: facebook.com/makesmthng

People for the Ethical Treatment of Animals (PETA): peta.org

Project 333: bemorewithless.com/project-333

United Students Against Sweatshops: usas.org

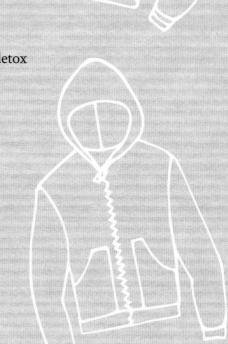

Film/Television

Minimalism: minimalismfilm.com

"Redress Design Award": youtube.com/RedressAsia

River Blue: riverbluethemovie.eco

The True Cost: truecostmovie.com

For a complete list of references, visit the page for this book on our website (orcabook.com).

Glossary

activists—people who campaign to bring about social, environmental or political change

boycott—refuse to buy goods as punishment or protest

catalyst—a substance that increases the rate of a chemical reaction

classes—groups of people defined by their social or economic status

climate change—a change in climate patterns largely attributed to the increased levels of carbon dioxide in the atmosphere, caused by the use of fossil fuels

consumerism—the pre-occupation with acquiring consumer goods

cultural appropriation—the adoption of elements of one culture by members of another culture without getting permission, giving credit or respecting the original culture or context

data—facts and statistics collected for reference or analysis

developmental delays—mental or physical delays in a child's development

disposable good—a product designed to be used once and then disposed of

domesticating—taming an animal to keep on a farm or in a home

fast fashion—inexpensive clothing produced quickly by chain retailers in response to the latest trends

fertilizers—substances used to make soil more fertile

fossil fuels—fuels formed in the earth from the decomposition of plants and animals

free trade agreements—agreements between two or more countries that reduce barriers to importing and exporting goods

gender stereotyping—reinforcing simplistic generalizations about people based on their gender

globalization—the spread of products, technology, information and jobs across national borders

greenhouse gases—gases that absorb infrared radiation and trap heat in the atmosphere

hashtag—a word or phrase preceded by a hash sign (#), used on social media websites and applications to identify messages on a specific topic

immigrants—people who move to a foreign country to live there permanently

looms—apparatuses used for weaving yarn or thread into fabric

microfibers—very fine synthetic fibers

outsourcing—the business practice of obtaining goods or services from an outside source, usually foreign suppliers

pesticides—substances used to destroy insects or other organisms harmful to plants or animals

petroleum—a liquid substance found in rocks that can be used to make fuels

refashion—remake

renewable resource—a resource that can be used repeatedly and never runs out because it's replaced naturally

social media—websites and applications that allow people to create and share content and participate in social networking

spindles—thin rods used for twisting natural fibers into thread

strike—a refusal to work organized by a union in an attempt to get an employer to make concessions

sumptuary laws—laws that limit how much people can spend on food and personal items

supply chains—the sequential processes involved in the production and distribution of goods

sustainable—able to be maintained at a certain rate or level

sweatshops—factories where people are employed at low wages and work long hours in poor conditions

synthetic—made through chemical processes

targeted advertising—a form of advertising that is directed at people with certain traits

thrifting—shopping at secondhand stores

unions—organized associations of workers formed to protect and further their rights and interests

unisex—suitable for all genders

wastewater—water that has been used as part of an industrial process

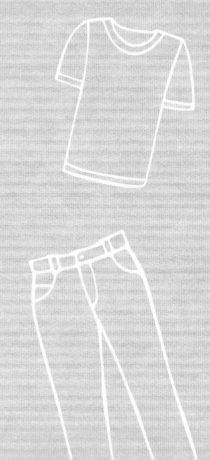

Index

Page numbers in **bold** indicate an image caption.

Index (continued)